Carving
Realistic
Flowers

REVISED EDITION

Wanda Marsh

FOX CHAPEL
PUBLISHING

© 2001, 2014 by Wanda Marsh and Fox Chapel Publishing Company, Inc., East Petersburg, PA.

Carving Realistic Flowers, Revised Edition (ISBN 978-1-56523-818-3, 2014) is a revised edition of *Carving Realistic Flowers in Wood* (ISBN 978-1-56523-154-2, 2001), published by Fox Chapel Publishing Company, Inc. The patterns contained herein are copyrighted by the author. Readers may make copies of these patterns for personal use. The patterns themselves, however, are not to be duplicated for resale or distribution under any circumstances. Any such copying is a violation of copyright law.

ISBN 978-1-56523-818-3

To learn more about the other great books from Fox Chapel Publishing, or to find a retailer near you, call toll-free 800-457-9112 or visit us at *www.FoxChapelPublishing.com*.

Note to Authors: We are always looking for talented authors to write new books. Please send a brief letter describing your idea to Acquisition Editor, 1970 Broad Street, East Petersburg, PA 17520.

Printed in China
First printing

Table of Contents

About the Author

Wanda Marsh began carving in 1993 in her native Texas. Many of her inspirations have come from watching the bird feeders she has placed outside her windows and the flowers that she has planted in her yard. Not to be limited to her own yard, she may even see something while traveling that sparks an idea.

Wanda's first attempts at flowers came less than a year after she first began carving. A friend suggested that she carve a rose for the Tyler Rose Show that she had planned to attend. The idea took root, and Wanda began researching books and taking photos of roses at nurseries. Many beautiful roses were dissected for the cause of a good carving. After finishing her first rose, her daughter suggested she place a loose petal on the base of the carving—a reference to the Beast's rose in *Beauty and the Beast.*

After carving the rose, Wanda's appetite for flower carving has been insatiable. She enjoys the challenge of seeing how she can make different flowers out of wood. Friends now get that knowing look when Wanda picks a flower and takes it home. They know that in many cases its likeness will be carved before it wilts, and quite possibly the carved version will win a ribbon along the way.

Editor's note: Don't be fooled into thinking that Wanda Marsh stops with flower carving. She is an award-winning carver of fish, animals and caricatures as well. Her awards include a sweep of the flower division at the 2000 International Woodcarvers Congress (morning glory first place; hibiscus, second place; and rose, third place) and a People's Choice Award for an iris at the Houston Area Woodcarvers Show. She holds other honors for fish carving from the Louisiana Wildfowl Carvers & Collectors Guild, the East Texas Woodcarvers Annual Show, the Killeen Centroplex Woodcarvers Show and the World Fish Carving Championship. A popular instructor, Wanda can be found teaching seminars in Texas and other nearby states.

Dedication

I would like to lovingly dedicate this book to my husband, Ronnie Marsh, and my nine grandchildren. Special thanks to Linda and Mike Hughes, Joan Brueggeman, Trudy Rossiter and Margaret Cawood for all their help and support.

Introduction

It is always more enjoyable to carve something you love, and I love flowers. My ongoing goal is to bring as much realism as I can to the flowers I carve. My passion for carving flowers has become a family act. My husband, Ronnie, and I search out flowers to carve. Ronnie keeps his camera handy whenever we visit nurseries, gardens and friends. Sometimes we have visited places so often to check out or photograph a flower that the owner just gives us the plant. This book is the result of many hours of effort in carving, painting and finishing to get the realism just right.

What I would like for you to learn from this book is not only how to carve flowers, but to actually see flowers and their leaves in a different way: the beauty of a leaf, the curves on a flower, the soft flow of each petal. We can see this best of all by looking at the natural beauty the Lord has already provided all around us.

I recommend that you take the time to begin with the morning glory project and follow up with the hibiscus before attempting the rose. The first two projects teach techniques that will help you to successfully carve the rose, which is the most advanced of these three projects. Use this book as a guide, and don't let it limit you to doing the same exact flower over and over. Do your own thing and, like nature itself, make each flower take on its own personality and shape.

I am thrilled to be passing these techniques and patterns on to you in this book. You can now share the joy I have found in carving these flowers and winning numerous awards for each. The fine detail that can be achieved here with power tools is sure to earn you compliments galore.

Wanda Marsh

Gallery

This single morning glory is carved by the author in the demonstration on page 13.

This red rose is carved by the author in the demonstration on page 41.

This salmon-colored hibiscus is carved by the author in the demonstration on page 27.

Bearded iris mounted on a burl knot. The bearded iris is one of the largest and more difficult flowers to carve.

A group of three pansies mounted on driftwood, which is then mounted on a red oak rectangular base. In this photo, the driftwood helps stabilize the pansies. These flowers are each done out of one piece of tupelo wood.

This gloxinia is fun to carve! It is a popular flower around Easter and Mother's Day. Try to give a soft, velvety look to the finished flower.

Classic Cattleya orchid mounted on a piece of driftwood. In all of your finished pieces be sure that the base you use does not overwhelm the flower.

Open lily and bud. The open lily is carved out of one piece of tupelo wood. The finished flowers are mounted on a piece of driftwood.

Grouping of five morning glories mounted on driftwood and an oval oak base. Notice that all the flowers are not facing forward, but are positioned in different profiles.

CHAPTER ONE

Getting Started

Carving flowers is a creative, yet humbling art. It takes a lot of patience and practice, but the end result is well worth the effort. Nothing is quite like the thrill of reproducing one of nature's flowers in wood. Of course, at times nothing is quite as frustrating either. The information presented in this chapter will help to get you started on carving flowers. Review it carefully before you begin the projects in this book.

Safety

Safety issues should always be first in your mind when you are carving. The flowers in this book are carved with power tools, so some extra safety precautions are warranted.

Know your tools. Whether you are new to power carving or an expert who just bought a new tool, take the time to become familiar with your tools before you begin carving. Take a class; practice on a piece of scrap wood; read the manual—these are all important ways to understand how the tools you are using will act or react in any given situation.

Understand the project. Take the time to review the carving demonstrations for the flowers in this book from start to finish. Reviewing all of the directions before you begin will give you a better idea of your goal and help you to avoid frustration.

Block out distractions. You need to be focused to carve well. Find a quiet area where interruptions will be limited. Gather all your materials in advance of the project so everything is at your fingertips. As I mentioned, flower carving takes time and patience. Blocking out distractions will help you focus.

Take breaks. On the other hand, don't become so focused that you forget to take a break every now and then. Your margin of safety decreases substantially as you become tired. Never carve while you are fatigued or taking medications that will hamper your focus. It is important to stay alert.

Collect dust. While all the other safety issues apply to both hand and power carvers, this one is exclusive to power carvers. Dust collection units are an important addition to your carving studio. Even more important is that you use them regularly. Carving with power tools creates lots of fine dust that you don't want to breathe.

Reference Material

To get you started, I have included reference photos of the rose, hibiscus and morning glory in this book. However, you'll probably want to gather more information about these flowers before you begin carving.

Botanical gardens, flower shops and gardening centers are great places to find reference material. You can take pictures of flowers that interest you and even buy plants to take home for live reference (and enjoyment).

Your local library, book stores and home improvement stores are also great places to find reference material. Many books are published each year on gardening, and a number of them will have beautiful, close-up photos of plants in bloom. Seed catalogs are another good source of reference.

If you have a computer and a connection to the Internet, check out the various flower societies that support websites. You'll also find a number of flower-growers who enjoy posting pictures of their prize plants on the web.

Flower Anatomy

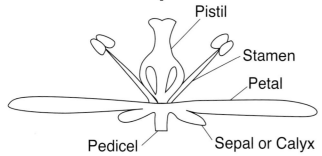

Tools

I use a flexible shaft machine for all of my power carving. These versatile machines allow you to quickly remove wood in a variety of ways. Some flexible shaft machines are designed to hang from a bracket; others remain stationary on a bench or table top. Make your choice based on the set-up of your carving studio. A sheathed flexible shaft connects the motor to any one of a variety of handpieces. Handpieces give the flexible shaft machines their versatility. You can choose from a large handpiece or a small handpiece, then change collets to accept a wide variety of differently shaped bits. Manufacturers of the flexible shaft machines also make handpieces.

Once you are set with a power carving tool, you'll need to choose bits and burs for your project. The basic ones that I recommend are listed at the beginning of the projects.

In addition, you'll need the following miscellaneous items.
- 220-grit sandpaper
- 400-grit sandpaper
- ⅜-inch drill bit for the center of the flowers
- compass
- super glue
- 16-gauge copper wire to attach leaves
- 18-gauge copper wire to make stems
- soldering iron to join leaves and stems
- two-part five-minute epoxy

Wood

My wood of choice is tupelo, though I started carving with basswood. I have found over the years that tupelo wood works better for flower carving for a number of reasons. 1) It does not "fuzz" when you carve it, which lessens the amount of sanding you need to do. 2) The grain is very close, allowing you to carve in any direction. 3) Sealers are not needed.

Tupelo may be hard to find. Most lumber stores and home improvement stores do not carry it. There are many wood carving supply stores that sell tupelo through mail-order catalogs and over the Internet. Check your local library for wood carving magazines that advertise these shops or do an Internet search for wood carving supplies.

Paint

Painting is crucial when finishing a flower. A heavy-handed paint job will destroy even the most beautifully carved flower. I use washes to achieve depth of color on the petals and the leaves without the heavy, unnatural-looking paint job

Washes are simply a thinned-down version of the paint. I mix acrylic paints with water to make the washes used on the flowers in this book. I have tried a variety of commercial thinners, but I find that water works the best.

Some areas of the flower are painted with acrylics used straight from the tube. Stamens, calyx and stems do not require thinned-down washes.

If you are using tupelo wood, sealing the wood before you paint it is not required. I find that I get a more natural, softer-looking finished flower if I don't use sealer or gesso prior to painting.

CHAPTER TWO

Power Carving
the Morning Glory

The results you can achieve carving the morning glory will astound you. With power tools and tupelo wood you can carve this flower to a delicate thinness. Part of the secret here is that the edges are thin while leaving a little more thickness on the rest of the flower. To carve this beautiful flower, let's first understand a little about it. Morning glories are decorative blooming vines that twine around fences, porch rails, and even other shrubs. Their prolific blooms announce the warmer weather of the summer months.

As its name suggests, the morning glory blossoms unfurl in the morning hours to greet the sun and then close later in the day as the sun gets hot. By evening, when temperatures are cooler, the blooms are tightly closed. Taking these facts in mind, you can see that you need to begin looking for a piece of driftwood or fence-type material to mount your finished project on as a vine, not a free-standing plant. Brilliant blue is the most common color for the morning glory's trumpet-shaped blossoms. Other varieties sport scarlet, pink and white, or multi-colored blooms. What follows on the next two pages are reference photos to aid you in understanding the shape, texture and colors of these delightful flowers.

SKILL LEVEL: Beginner

FINISHED SIZE: 2½ inch diameter

TIP: Practice. The techniques used to carve this flower can be used to carve virtually any flower with great success.

Morning Glory Reference Photos

Morning Glory Pattern

Morning Glory
top view

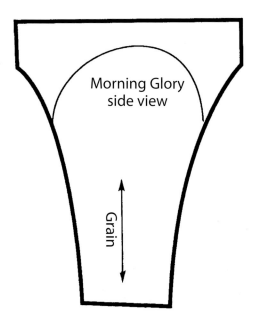

Morning Glory
side view

Grain

Mark the center point of the top view and drill a hole 1¾ in. deep by ⅜ in. wide. Use tupelo wood for the best results.

Note: Don't limit your carving to flowers this size. Vary the diameter and depth of your cutouts to make interesting arrangements.

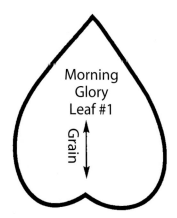

Morning Glory Leaf #1

Grain

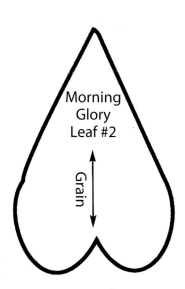

Morning Glory Leaf #2

Grain

Cut the leaves out of ½-inch-thick tupelo, varying the shape and size of each leaf. I use at least three leaves for one flower.

Carving the Morning Glory

Use the reference photos and information on the previous pages and the pattern on page 12 to design your flower. Read all carving instructions before beginning the project. You'll need a block of tupelo wood 2½ inches by 2½ inches by 3 inches tall for the flower. The leaves are carved from tupelo wood that measures 1½ inches by 1½ inches by ¼ inch thick.

Assemble the following tools and materials:

- soft sanding drum
- ¼-in. roll sanding mandrel
- ⅛-in. round shank burr
- ⅛-in. tapered shank burr
- tapered diamond carver
- long tapered diamond carver
- 220- and 400-grit sandpaper
- compass
- 12-gauge copper wire
- ³⁄₆₄-in. solid brass rods
- super glue

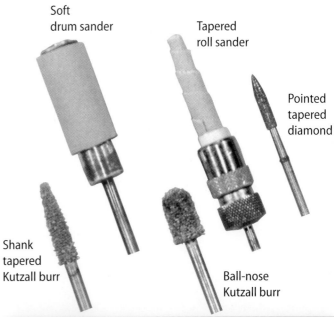

Soft drum sander

Tapered roll sander

Pointed tapered diamond

Shank tapered Kutzall burr

Ball-nose Kutzall burr

Preparing the Block

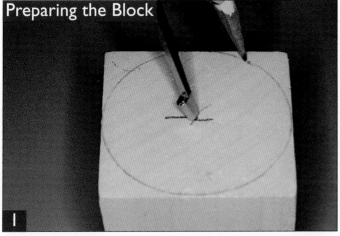

1 Draw a circle on top of the block of wood with a compass. On the bottom of the wood, draw intersecting lines to mark the center point on the bottom of the block. This center point is an important mark. Use it as a guide to keep the center of the flower in line with the base.

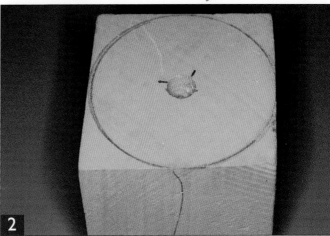

2 In the center of the circle, drill a hole ⅜ inch wide and 1¼ inches deep. The pencil line on the side of the block indicates the direction of the grain.

3 Cut the circle out on a band saw. Draw a star on the top to mark the five sections of the flower. Don't worry about making the star perfectly symmetrical. It is simply a guide. Draw a line from the point of the star to the hole you drilled in the center. Do this for each of the five sections.

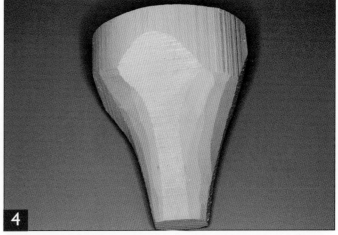

4 Use a band saw to cut the waste wood from the side of the flower. Taper the blank to a 1-inch diameter on the bottom.

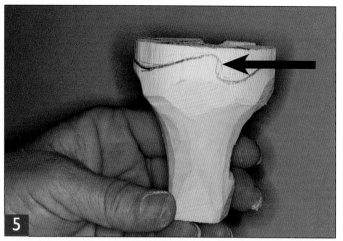

5

Draw a wavy line near the top of the blank. The lower parts of the wave should fall under the points of the star that you drew in Step 3. This will mark the edge of the flower. Be sure to turn some curves and vary the line to add interest to the flower.

Shaping the Top of the Flower

6

Use a tapered bur to make a groove from the center to the point of each star. Be sure to round off the groove where it meets the hole at the center of the flower. You want to avoid having a sharp, 90-degree drop into the flower's center.

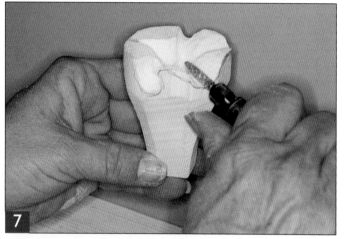

7

Still using a tapered bur, expand the grooves to match the wavy lines on the outside of the flower. Notice the depth of the cuts and how the cuts taper into the center of the flower.

8

Continue working all around the top of the flower to bring the wood down to the wavy line.

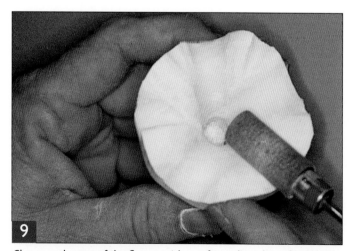

9

Clean up the top of the flower with a soft sanding drum fitted with 220 grit sandpaper. Follow the grooves and cuts that you made with the tapered bur.

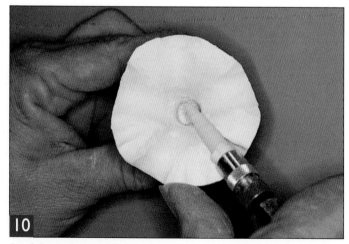

10

Sand the center and the hard-to-reach areas with a ¼-inch sanding roll or a tapered diamond carver. It is important that the wood is sanded as smoothly as possible before you move on to the next step.

11

Draw a star pattern on the five lower parts of the flower. Draw a single line radiating from the center on the higher parts of the flower. This represents the basic pattern found in a morning glory.

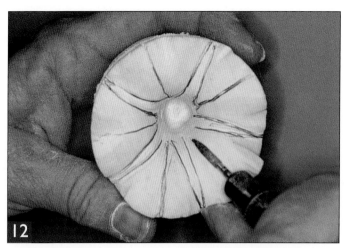

12

Score all the lines lightly with a long tapered diamond carver.

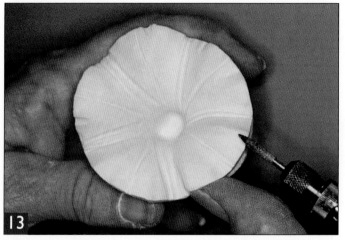

13

When you are finished scoring the lines, the flower will look like this.

14

Draw lines that radiate from the score marks you made on the high points of the flower top. Score these lightly with a tapered bit. These cuts will give texture to the surface of the flower.

Shaping the Underside of the Flower

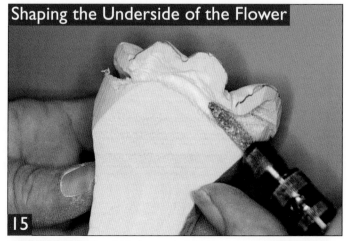

15

Using the tapered carbide bur, carve all the way around the flower edge, about ¼ inch down from the top of the flower. Don't cut any closer to the flower at this point.

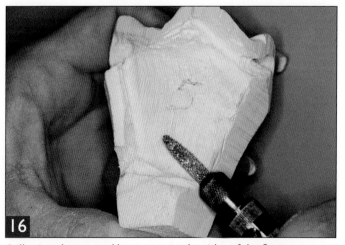

16

Still using the tapered bur, cut away the sides of the flower as shown. Leave about ¾ of an inch of wood on the bottom of the flower. This will give you a piece of wood to hold as you carve. (The number 5 helps Wanda keep track of the petals).

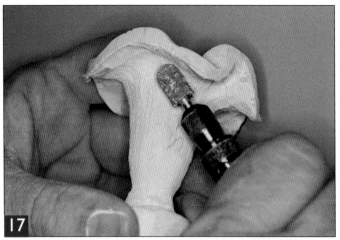

17

Take the round bur and shape the curved areas under the petal edges on the upper part of the flower. Don't go any thinner than ¼ inch at this point. Some additional wood will be removed during the sanding process in Step 18.

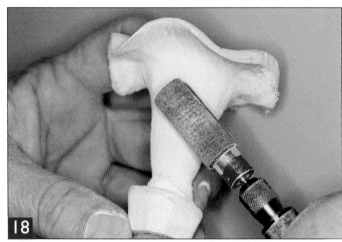

18

Clean up the underside of the flower with a soft drum sander equipped with 220-grit sandpaper. Follow up with 400-grit sandpaper. Make the wood as smooth as possible before you move on to the next step.

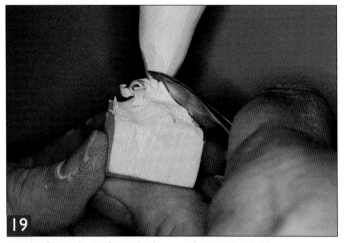

19

Cut the flower loose from the base with a carving knife or a tapered bur.

20

The flower is removed from the base.

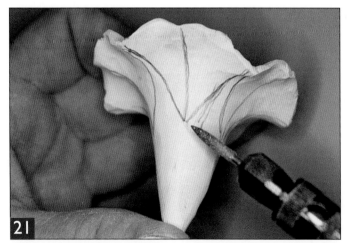

21

On the underside of the flower, draw the same star-shaped pattern and straight lines that you drew on the top of the flower in Step 11. The points of the star mark the lowest level of the flower edge; the lines mark the highest level of the flower edge. Score each line with a diamond point bit.

22

Study your reference material, then draw a five pointed sepal on the bottom of the flower. Notice the additional vein lines that were added to the underside of the flower with a diamond point bit. These radiate from the score lines that were carved in Step 21.

23 Score along the line for the sepal with a diamond point bit.

Adding the Stamens

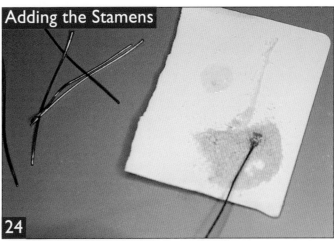

24 Cut five 1¼-long pieces of 12-gauge stranded copper wire. Put glue on the tips and roll the wire in sawdust to create the illusion of pollen. These pieces of wire will form the flower stamens.

25 Twist the bottoms of the wires together (about ½ inch). Trim the copper to fit the flower, leaving room to insert the twisted section into the wood. The stamens, when inserted, should not extend above the flower.

26 Drill a hole in the center of the flower. Double check the height of the stamens. Wait to glue the stamens in place until the flower has been painted.

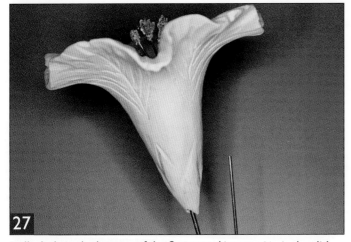

27 Drill a hole in the bottom of the flower and insert a ³⁄₆₄-inch solid brass rod. This rod will form the stem of the flower. Wait to glue the stem in place until the flower has been painted.

Making the Leaves

28 Cut a heart shape from a piece of tupelo wood 1½ inches by 1½ inches by ¼ inch thick to form the leaf. Cut at least three leaves, varying the shape and size of each.

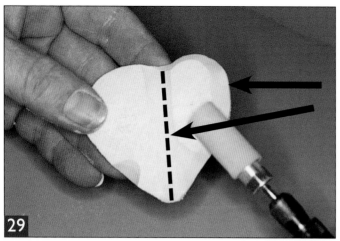

29 Use a drum sander to round off the top edges. Make a soft, shallow groove down the center of the leaf. This will form the top side of the leaf.

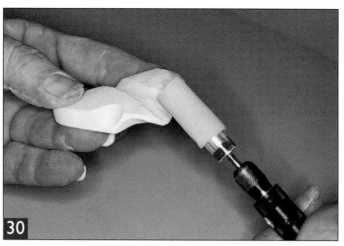

30 To make the leaves realistic, carve gentle folds with the sanding drum. Be creative and do each leaf a little differently. The edges of the leaves should be sharp and as thin as possible; the center of the leaf is about ⅛ inch thick. Check your work frequently by holding the leaf in front of a strong light. The light will shine through the thin areas.

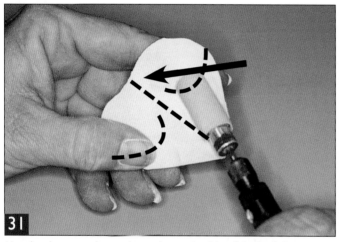

31 Use the drum sander to shape the underside of the leaf. Create a shallow concave appearance by removing a small amount of wood on the left and right sides of the leaf.

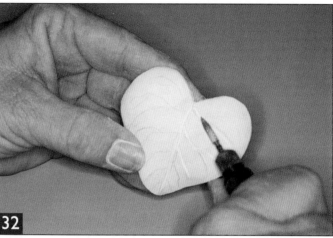

32 Check your reference material and use a pointed diamond bit to make light indentations on the top of the leaf for the veins. The most prominent indentation should run down the center of the leaf. Additional lines should run from the center line out to the edge of the leaf.

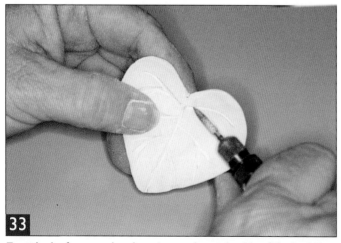

33 Turn the leaf over and make veins on the underside of the leaf. Use the same process as described in Step 32.

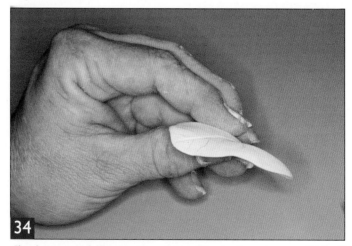

34 Check your work. Be sure the edges of the leaf are sharp and thin. If not, go back to Step 30 and reshape the leaf.

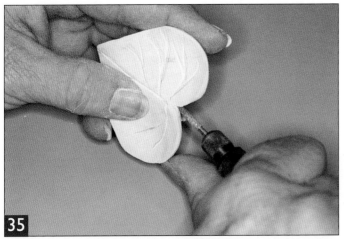

35

When you are satisfied with the appearance of the leaf, drill a small hole in the center edge of the leaf. Insert a ³⁄₆₄-inch brass rod to form the stem. Wait to glue the stem in place until the flower has been painted.

36

A top view of the carved morning glory and leaf. Take the time to match your pieces to these views before moving on to the painting section of this demonstration.

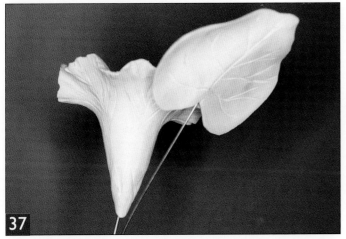

37

Note the detail that has been added to the underside of the leaf and flower. These score lines mimic the veins found in real flowers and add realism to the carved version. The leaf stems are soldered to the main stem.

38

A side view of the carved morning glory and leaf.

Painting the Morning Glory

Once your flower has been carved and shaped and sanded smooth, you are ready to paint. I do not seal my flowers before painting beccause I use tupelo wood. If you are using basswood, you may wish to use sealer. Refer to the general painting instructions in the beginning of this book for specific information on acrylic painting techniques. The washes mentioned in the demonstration are created by mixing paint with water until a thin-consistency wash is formed. Reference material will play a big role in painting. Use the photos of the live plant on pages 10-11 or gather your own. You will need to following paints and brushes:

- narrow flat brush
- wide flat brush
- #0/#10 liner brush
- Jo Sonja All-Purpose Sealer
- Krylon Matte Finish
- super glue
- Jo Sonja acrylic paints (listed at right)

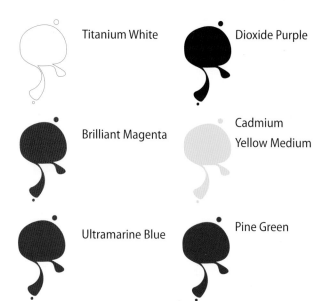

Titanium White

Dioxide Purple

Brilliant Magenta

Cadmium Yellow Medium

Ultramarine Blue

Pine Green

Painting the Flower

1 Paint three washes of titanium white inside the hole at the center of the flower. Pull the color out onto the petals in a star pattern as shown above. Allow the paint to dry before moving on to the next step.

2 Make a magenta wash. Starting toward the outside of the petals, pull color into the white paint that you added in Step 1.

3 Paint three thin washes of titanium white on the outside star shape. Do not paint the sepal. Allow the paint to dry. Then add a magenta wash, pulling from the outside in as you did in Step 2.

4 Thin ultramarine blue with water and pull paint from the outside of the flower petal into the magenta wash done in step 2. You will be painting over most of the magenta color. You may need more than one wash to get the correct coverage.

5 Still using the ultramarine blue, repeat the blue wash on the underside of the flower.

6 Add a touch of dioxide purple to the ultramarine blue wash to paint the shadow areas. Paint a faint touch of cadmium yellow medium, straight from the tube, in the bottom of the hole in the center of the flower.

7 Paint the shadow areas on the underside of the flower with the same ultramarine blue/dioxide purple mixture that you used in Step 6. Paint the calyx a pine green wash. Use cadmium yellow medium on the tips of the calyx to create highlights.

8 Paint three pine green base coat washes. Three thin coats will give you a nice, even color.

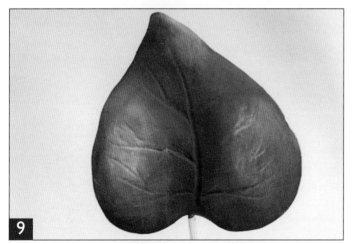

9 While the base coat is still wet, highlight the high points of the leaves with cadmium yellow medium. Adding the yellow highlights while the green paint is still wet will keep the yellow from looking too strong.

10 Make a wash of 60 percent cadmium yellow medium and 40 percent pine green wash to accent the veins on the leaf. Using a liner brush, carefully follow the lines you scored with the diamond bit.

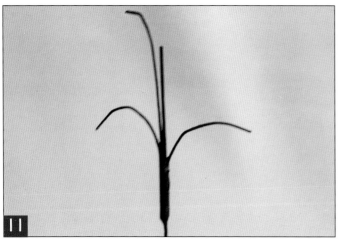

11

Before soldering, apply two coats of all-purpose metal sealer to the stems. Allow the sealer to dry completely. Then paint the stems with pine green straight from the tube.

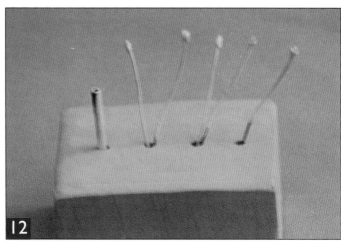

12

Paint the stamens with all-purpose metal sealer, then color them with titanium white. I will be adding a hummingbird to my carving. The 3/32-inch tubing (shown on the left) will hold the hummingbird in place.

13

Use super glue to secure all of the pieces.

Finishing Touches

I like to use a finished base and a piece of driftwood to display my morning glory. Vary your arrangements by adding hummingbirds or additional flowers and leaves. Try to be sure that your base and driftwood do not overpower the delicate beauty of your finished flowers. Coat the finished piece with a light spray of protective matte finish, such as Krylon Matte Finish. Be careful to use a light spray. A heavy spray coat may make the finished piece shiny and unnatural. (See more photos of the finished carving on page 2.)

CHAPTER THREE

Power Carving
the Hibiscus

Let's take a departure from the vining morning glory and carve the tropical hibiscus. The hibiscus is a larger flower that has some varieties with blooms as large as 14 inches or more in diameter. This is a plant that thrives naturally in warmer tropical climates. It is a sturdy plant in contrast to the vining morning glory that you just finished. It does have many of the carving characteristics of the morning glory, though, just on a bigger scale.

Again, the next few pages contain reference photos to help you in your carving. As for colors, the array of colors of hibiscus are great. You might want to consider the popular red hibiscus or experiment with yellow, pink, white, mauve, even brown! Once you begin to explore the possibilities, you will be astounded at the wide array of colors of hibiscus! After you pick a color, look at the many types of petals and sizes. Use these instructions as a guide to help you. Notice that in nature, sizes vary, the ruffles vary, even the colors vary. Growers of hibiscus are frequently amazed, when they try to hybridize a hibiscus, at the color or shape they end up with.

Because this is a larger flower, you may consider doing only one or several in your finished carving arrangement. If you want to add a bit of carving fun, add a lady bug, a butterfly or a bee.

SKILL LEVEL: Beginner

FINISHED SIZE: 2½ inch diameter

TIP: Practice. The techniques used to carve this flower can be used to carve virtually any flower with great success.

Hibiscus Reference Photos

Hibiscus Pattern

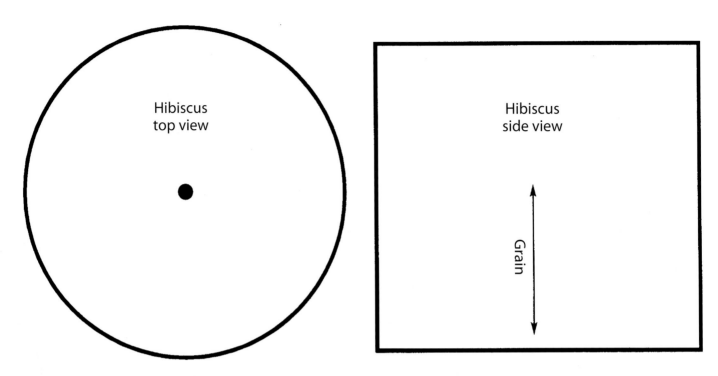

Mark the center point of the top view. Drill a hole 2½ inches deep and ¼ inch wide at this mark. Use tupelo wood for the best results.

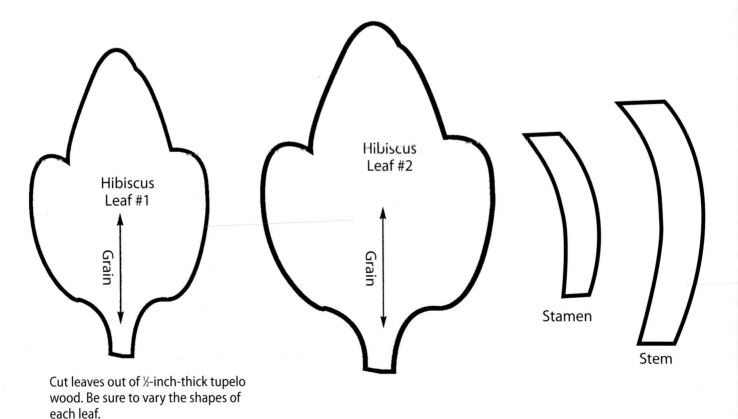

Cut leaves out of ½-inch-thick tupelo wood. Be sure to vary the shapes of each leaf.

© WANDA MARSH

Carving the Hibiscus

Use the pattern on page 26 and the reference material at the beginning of this chapter to plan your hibiscus flower. You will need a block of tupelo wood 3¼ inches by 3¼ inches by 3½ inches high. The leaves are carved from ½-inch pieces of scrap wood. The stem and the stamens are carved from 2½-inch-long pieces of wood. Assemble the following tools:

- ball-nosed Kutzall
- tapered Kutzall
- tapered ruby carver
- diamond tapered bit
- drum sander
- tapered sander
- round disc carver

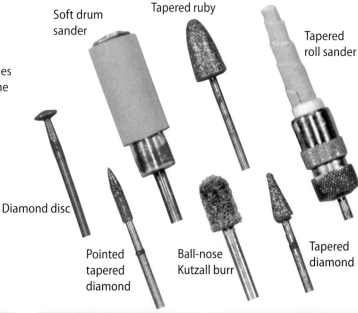

Soft drum sander

Tapered ruby

Tapered roll sander

Diamond disc

Pointed tapered diamond

Ball-nose Kutzall burr

Tapered diamond

Preparing the Block

1 Draw a circle on top of a block of wood 3¼ inches by 3¼ inches by 3½ inches high. Mark the center point of the circle and drill a ¼-inch-wide and 2½-inch-deep hole at this mark.

2 Turn the block over and mark the center point on the bottom of the wood. Then cut away the waste wood on a band saw.

3 Divide the circumference into five equal parts. Use a band saw to cut the waste wood from the side of the flower, tapering the wood to a 1-inch-diameter at the base.

Shaping the Top of the Flower

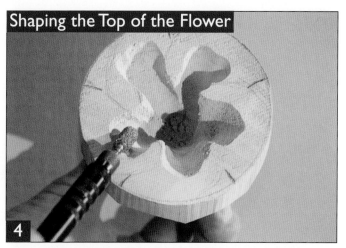

4 Using a ball-nosed Kutzall, hollow out the wood between the five marks. The hollowed out area is roughly 2½ inches deep at the center.

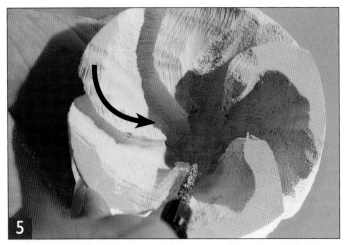

5

With a tapered Kutzall, cut a swirl pattern to form five petals. Taper each petal, as the arrow shows, toward the center of the flower.

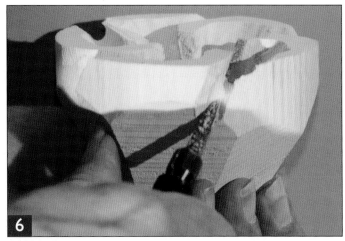

6

Separate the petals by continuing the cuts from Step 5 down the side of the flower.

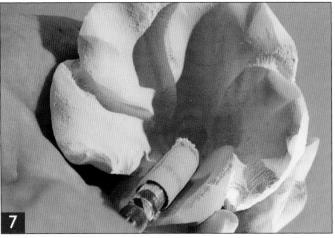

7

Use a drum sander fitted with 220-grit sandpaper to sand away the marks on the top of the flower.

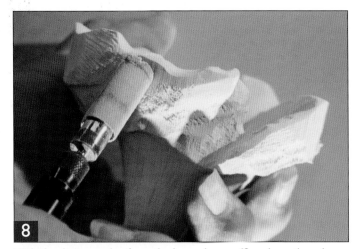

8

With the drum sander, form the large deep ruffles along the edge of the hibiscus.

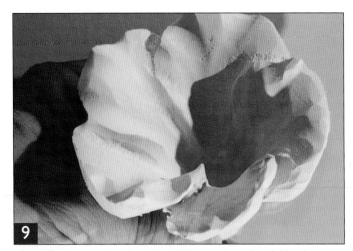

9

The ruffles are now in place. Your hibiscus should look like this before you proceed to the next step.

10

Using a ruby tapered bit, make the smaller ruffles all the way around the edges of the hibiscus.

A side view photograph shows the indentations of the ruffles.

Clean up the inside of the hibiscus with a drum sander and 400-grit sandpaper.

Use a tapered sander to clean between the ruffles.

Use a diamond taper bit to draw in lines and veins from the center of the hibiscus to its edges. Do not make the lines straight.

Shaping the Underside of the Flower

With a ball-nosed Kutzall, begin shaping the outer part of the hibiscus. Taper the sides down to the bottom.

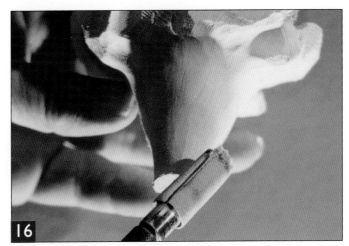

Use a drum sander with 220-grit sandpaper to clean up the outside of the hibiscus.

17

Make the petal separations on the outside of the hibiscus with a ruby taper.

18

With a ruby taper, begin taking away the bulk wood on the back side of the petals. Match the shape here to the top of each petal.

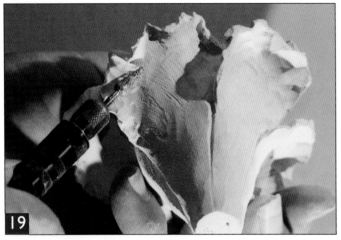

19

Use the ruby taper to make small ruffles on the underside edges of the petals.

20

Add vein lines to the underside of the flower with a round disc carver. These cuts should be shallow. Check your reference material to understand how the vein lines run.

21

Use a drum sander equipped with 220-grit sandpaper to sand the bottom of the flower to a point.

22

Draw the two sets of calyx on the bottom of the hibiscus. Check your reference material. The calyx at the very base of the flower is smaller than the calyx above it. Each calyx has five points.

23 Drag the pointed taper diamond bit across the surface of the wood to create a separation between the hibiscus and each set of calyx.

24 Lightly sand the flower with 400-grit sandpaper.

Stamens and Stems

25 Drill a small hole in the center of the finish-carved hibiscus to accommodate the flower stamens. Do not drill this hole all the way through the flower.

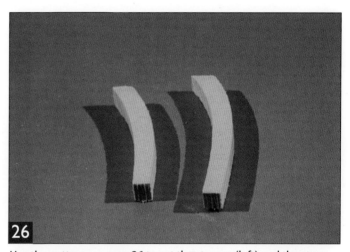

26 Use the pattern on page 26 to cut the stamen (left) and the stem (right). The stamen measures 1¾ inches by ¼ inches by ¼ inches. The stem measures 2½ inches by ½ inches by ½ inches. Slightly curve both stamen and stem.

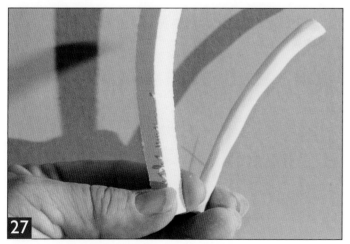

27 Use a sander to shape the stem until it is completely rounded

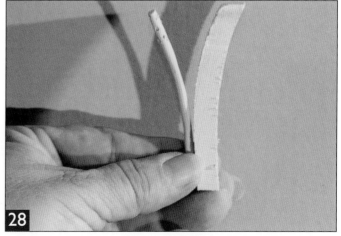

28 Round off the stamen with a sander. Drill a very small hole in the top for the pistils.

29

Drill a small hole in the bottom of the hibiscus flower and in the stem. Connect the hibiscus to the stem with a ³/₆₄-inch brass rod. Do not glue the pieces in place until the parts have been painted.

Making the Leaves

30

If you have access to real hibiscus leaves, use them as patterns. If not, use the patterns on page 26. Trace the leaf shapes on to ½-inch pieces of tupelo scrap wood and cut them out on a band saw.

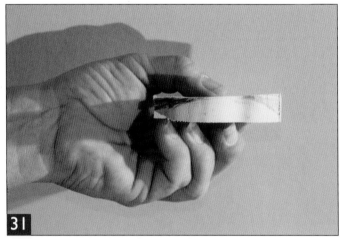

31

With a drum sander, remove wood from the front and the back of the blank to give some curvature to the leaf.

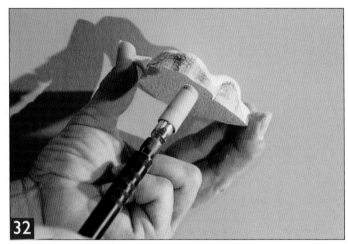

32

Use the drum sander with 220-grit sandpaper to make ruffles on the top side of the leaf.

33

Nothing beats the real hibiscus leaf as reference material. Compare your work to the real leaf or reference photos. When you are satisfied with the shape, sand the bottom of the leaf to match the top.

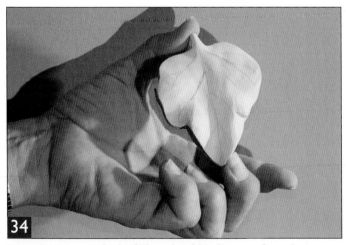

34

Draw the veins on the leaf. They should radiate out from the center line of the leaf. Again, refer to your reference material.

35

Drag the diamond taper along the lines to score the veins.

36

A close-up shot of the leaf shows the vein work. Notice how the major veins are scored deeper than the minor veins.

37

Use the disc to score the veins on the underside of the leaf. Because of the leaf's concave shape, the disc is easier to use here.

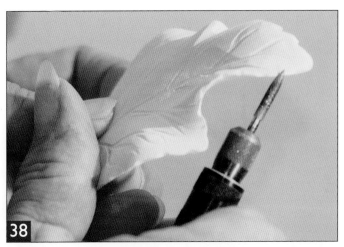

38

With the pointed taper, carve the scalloped edges around the leaf. Use an in-and-out motion to round off the edges.

39

Three finish-carved leaves are shown with actual hibiscus leaves. A ³⁄₆₄-inch brass rod is inserted into the base of each leaf for connection to the stem.

40

Drill small holes into the stem at different levels and insert the leaves. Refer to your reference material as you place the leaves. Note that hibiscus leaves are not directly opposite each other on the stem.

Painting the Hibiscus

As with the morning glory, I always use three base coats and allow them to dry between coats. I also don't use a sealant on tupelo wood. Hibiscus flowers come in a rainbow of colors. For this project, I am painting the flower a salmon pink color. If this does not match your decor or preference, check your reference material or visit a nursery to look at live plants for additional color options. The following Jo Sonja paints and materials are used in this demonstration:

- narrow flat brush
- wide flat brush
- #0/#10 liner brush
- super glue
- Krylon matte spray
- Jo Sonja acrylic paints (listed at right)

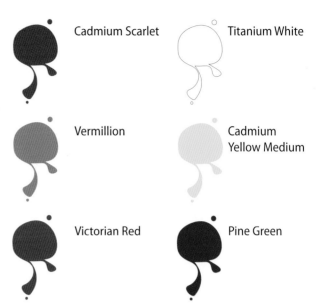

Cadmium Scarlet

Titanium White

Vermillion

Cadmium Yellow Medium

Victorian Red

Pine Green

Painting the Flower

1 Create a base coat wash by thinning vermillion and cadmium scarlet with water until you achieve a pleasing salmon color. Paint the entire underside of the flower with this mixture. Allow the paint to dry, then give the flower two more coats.

2 Using the same color wash, give the inside of the flower three coats of paint. Be sure to allow each coat to dry thoroughly before adding the next coat.

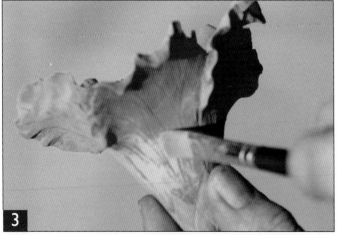

3 Mix cadmium scarlet and a small amount of white to make a slightly lighter tint. Dry brush this color across the underside of the flower. When dry brushing, always use undiluted paints and dry the brush off on a paper towel to remove the excess paint. Apply two or three coats, but do not paint so heavily that the darker-colored veining does not show through the lighter coats of paint.

4 Mix white and a touch a cadmium scarlet. Using the same techniques from Step 3, dry brush color across the petals to add highlights to the inside of the flower. Allow each coat to dry thoroughly before adding the next coat. Again, apply two or three coats, but be careful not to fill in the veins with the lighter paint.

5 Paint the base hole in the center of the flower with several wash coats of Victorian red. Using a pointed liner brush, pull the paint up each petal to form a feathered scallop shape as shown in the picture.

6 Use the liner brush and watered-down cadmium scarlet to lightly enhance the veins on the inside of the flower.

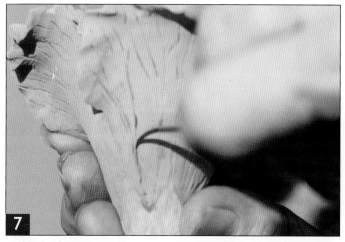

7 Highlight the veins on the underside of the flower using the same methods from Step 6.

8 Paint three coats of pine green wash on the calyx. While the last coat of green is still wet, blend cadmium yellow medium into the tips. Before the paint dries, separate the calyx from the flower with thinned-down white paint.

9 Paint the stamen with a wash mixture of vermillion and cadmium scarlet. Touch the bottom tips with full-strength yellow and the top four or five tips with full-strength red.

10 Paint the leaves and the stem of the hibiscus using the same techniques from the morning glory demonstration. (See page 21.) Allow all the parts to dry and assemble the flower. Lightly spray the finished arrangement with Krylon matte finish. (See more photos of the finished flower on page 4.)

CHAPTER FOUR

Power Carving
the Rose

The rose will be carved in three sections: the center, the middle, and outer sections. I feature the classic rose in the following instructions, but once you've learned how to do this rose, it will be easy to adapt what you've learned to carve any of the more than 2,000 species of roses. With all of these varieties to choose from you can have fun carving roses for a long time to come. These instructions will show how I carve the award-winning roses I've done for the carving show in Tyler, Texas, the rose capital of the world.

As in the previous two chapters, the next few pages contain reference photos of a few of these varieties. As you can see from the photos of my rose carvings, I like to nestle my roses on an attractive piece of driftwood, however, be creative and try other ways of displaying your rose as well. Be sure to let your rose be the main attraction when you mount your finished carving. Don't let your piece of driftwood or base overpower all of your hard work. As for your rose carvings, you might like to try adding rose buds, roses with more open centers, single roses (roses with just a single row of petals), smaller roses, etc. I even finished one of my roses like the rose from *Beauty and the Beast* with a fallen petal.

Common colors for roses are red, white, yellow—these are the most popular colors. Pink, salmon and even lavender, multi-colored and "black" varieties are available. If you are carving this project for a particular placement, you might consider a color that complements the decor. Whatever color or type of rose you choose to do, enjoy this project! I have found it very rewarding.

SKILL LEVEL: Advanced

FINISHED SIZE: 4-inch diameter

TIP: The rose is carved in three parts. Study side views of the live plant to ensure that the three parts nest in a natural-looking way.

Rose Reference Photos

Rose Pattern

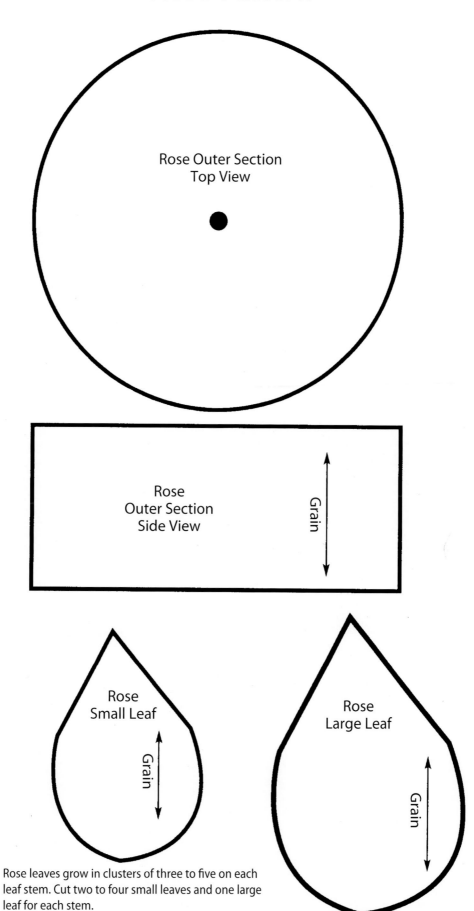

Rose Outer Section
Top View

Rose
Outer Section
Side View

Grain

Rose
Small Leaf

Grain

Rose
Large Leaf

Grain

Rose leaves grow in clusters of three to five on each leaf stem. Cut two to four small leaves and one large leaf for each stem.

© WANDA MARSH

Rose Pattern

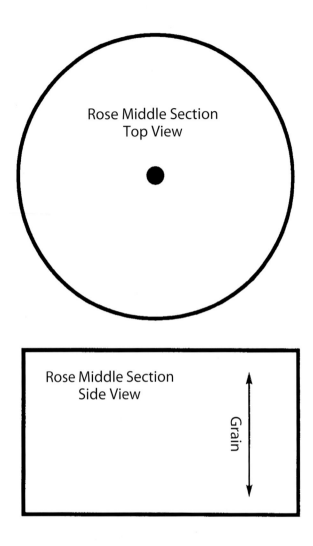

Rose Middle Section
Top View

Rose Middle Section
Side View

Grain

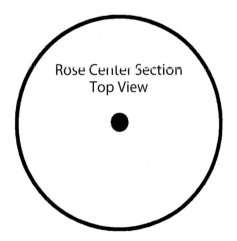

Rose Center Section
Top View

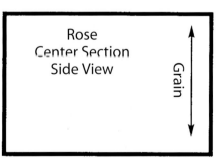

Rose
Center Section
Side View

Grain

Carving the Rose

The rose is carved in three sections: the center section, the middle section, and the outer section. The three sections nest together to form the completed rose. You'll need a block of tupelo wood 2½ inches by 2½ inches by 1⅜ inches tall for the center section. The middle section is carved from a 3 by 3 by 2-inch block. Carve the outer section from a 4 by 4 by 2-inch block. The leaves are carved from scrap wood. Read all the instructions and assemble your tools before beginning.

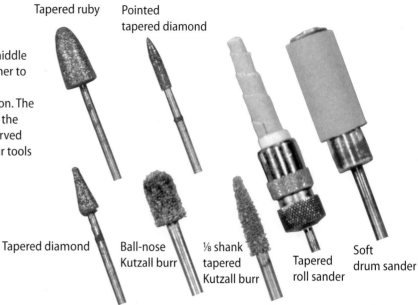

Tapered ruby

Pointed tapered diamond

Tapered diamond

Ball-nose Kutzall burr

⅛ shank tapered Kutzall burr

Tapered roll sander

Soft drum sander

Carving the Center Section

We begin by carving the center-most section of the flower. This section is the most important section when carving the rose. Take your time and really look at the reference photos to achieve a natural-looking rose. Do not try to get this section too thin at this time. You can thin it down later after all of the handling and fitting is done for the next section.

Study this photograph of the block and the carved center section. It is important to understand the shape you are trying to achieve before you begin cutting.

1

Draw the petal pattern on the block. Use a pointed ruby carver to make a small shallow hole no more than ¹⁄₁₆ inch deep in the center of the block.

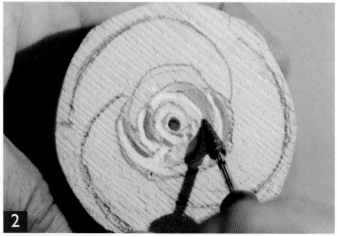

2

On the top of the block, use a medium grit, tapered ruby to form approximately six C-shaped cuts around the center hole. Each C-shaped cut should overlap the cut behind it.

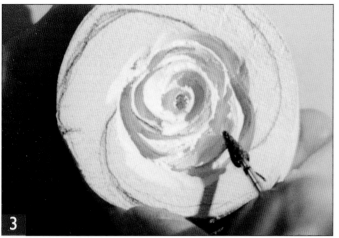

Round off and lower the edges of each C-shape to begin forming the petals.

Cut in to begin forming the larger outer petals of this section. Each petal is staggered behind the preceding petal.

Continue the cuts made in Step 4 down the side of the flower. Make each petal curve gently behind the petal in front.

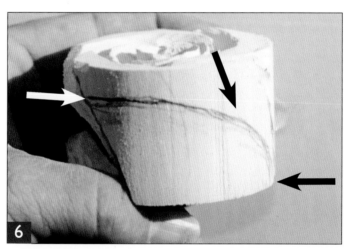

Draw three arcs on the side, one arc for each outer petal. The top of the arc should be at least ¼ inch from the top. Start the arc along the cut made in Step 5. The arc should end at the bottom of each cut.

With a Kutzall bur, remove the waste wood under the arcs you drew in Step 6. Taper the wood from the arc toward the bottom of the flower.

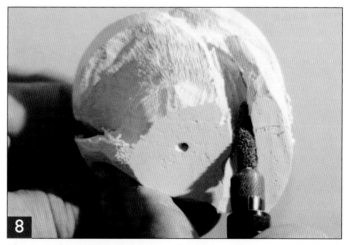

The taper forms a gentle backward "S" shape that narrows to about ¾ inch at the bottom of the flower. Note: The small drill hole on the base of the flower marks the center point of the rose.

9

Clean up the cuts at the top of the petals. Be sure to leave enough wood at the top of each petal for the ruffles that will be added later.

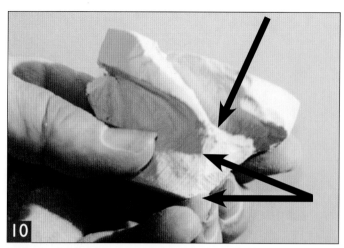

10

Smooth off the ridge at the edges of the lower half-inch of the petals. Taper the portion of the ridge just above this area to blend in.

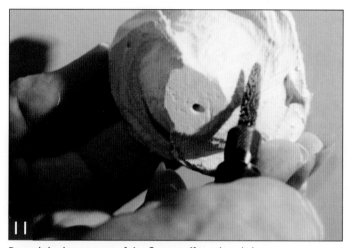

11

Round the lower part of the flower off to a bowl shape.

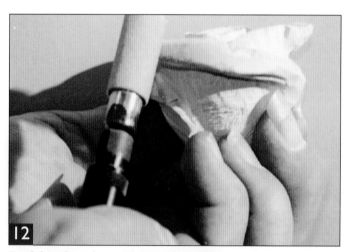

12

Sand the edges clean with 220-grit sandpaper.

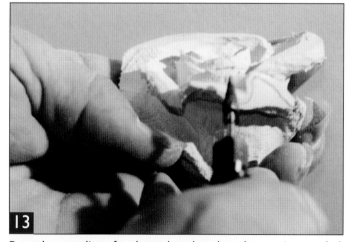

13

Draw the wavy line of each petal on the edges that you just sanded. Cut down to the line with a tapered ruby. Be sure to vary the wave on each petal. (The bottom edges will be cut in Step 16.)

14

Stop to check your work. The lower part of the flower and the edges of the petals should look like this.

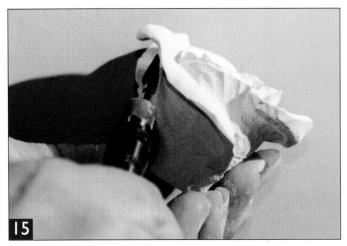

15 Use a tapered ruby to clean up between the sides of the petals.

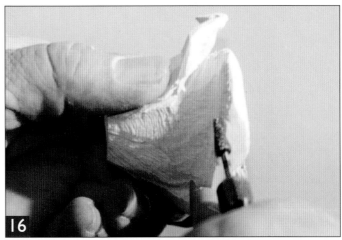

16 Still using the tapered ruby, cut the bottom edge of the petal to match the shape of the ruffle you cut in on the top edge of the petal.

17 Use a tapered diamond to clean up the small areas between the petals in the center of the rose. Hold your piece up to the light frequently to check for thin areas. Circle very thin areas with a pencil to remind yourself to avoid these sections.

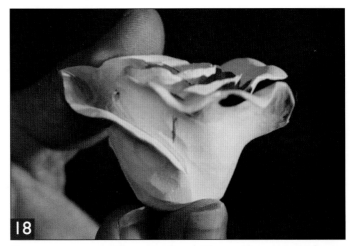

18 Compare your carved flower to the real flower. Your progress from a side view should look like this. Are the edges of your carved flower sharp and thin?

19 A view from the top of the finish-carved center. Note the delicate curving shape of the petals.

Carving the Middle Section

In this part of the demonstration, I'll show you how to carve the middle section of the rose. The center section will fit snugly inside this section when I'm finished.

Make this section with three or four carved petals. The number of petals is not as important as uniformity in size. Care needs to be taken to make the center section fit snugly into this middle section. It is very important to take your time with this section. This is the point where many carvers falter and end up with roses that have a pyramid shape, and not the gentle arching shape of a real rose. Take your time, removing little by little to match the dips and curves from this section to those of the center section that you just completed.

Study this photograph of the block and the carved middle section. It is important to understand the shape you are trying to achieve before you begin cutting.

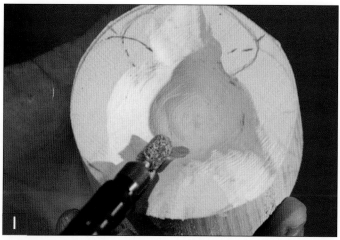

Using a ball-nosed Kutzall, round out the middle section. Your goal is to carve out an area to begin fitting the center section.

Place the finish-carved center section in the hollow area. Make a light reference mark on each section. This will allow you to line up the sections in the same positions as you continue to fit the pieces together.

The petals of the center section will act as guidelines showing you where to lower and remove wood from the middle section. Number the petals on the side of the block.

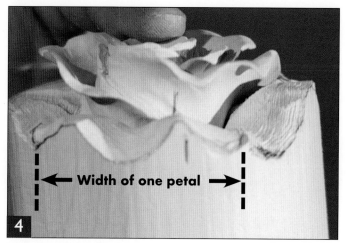

← Width of one petal →

Use a Kutzall to ruffle the petals. Continue to check the fit of the center piece. Remember to line up the reference marks for each fitting.

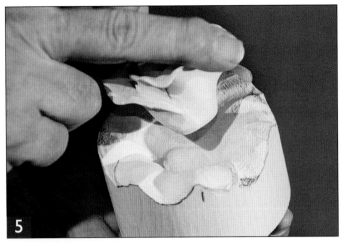

A look at the block at this point shows how the petals are beginning to flow over into the center.

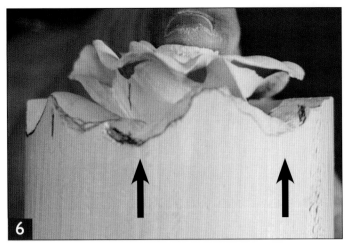

I have decided to make the center of this petal higher by cutting away wood from the petals on both sides. Notice that the fit is still not complete.

I have taken off more wood to make the fit better. Notice how the finished portion is being integrated into the middle section. This fit is closer to being correct.

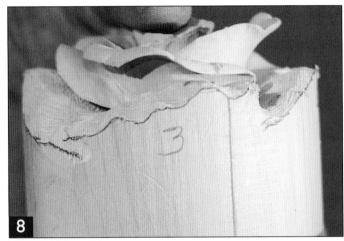

Decide how you want the petals to overlap and draw a wavy line on the side of the block to indicate ruffles. Cut the ruffles in with a Kutzall.

Make the ruffles on petal four different from the preceding petals. Remember, no two petals on the rose should be identical.

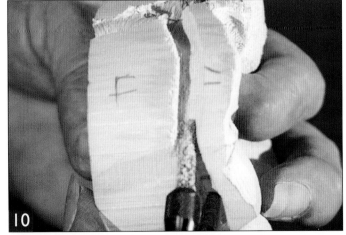

Cut a groove ¼ inch down from the top of the petals. Remove the waste wood from the side of the block with a tapered Kutzall bur as you did in Steps 5 to 8 of the center section.

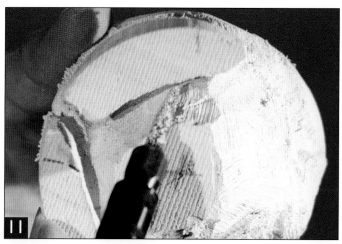

11

In this bottom view of the flower, you can see how the wood is being removed from the sides of the petals. Strive for a gentle bowl shape.

12

Real rose petals are great reference material. Here, I am using a real rose petal to help me form the shapes of the petals in this section.

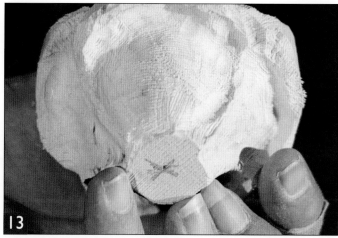

13

Cut the bottoms of the petals, making sure to keep the gentle bowl shape.

14

Use a drum sander with 220-grit sandpaper to clean up the marks from the Kutzall. This sanding will also thin the petals some, but not to their final thickness.

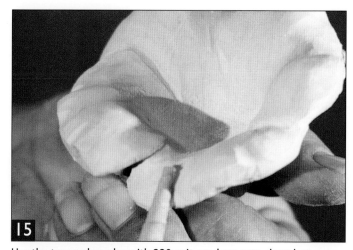

15

Use the tapered sander with 220-grit sandpaper to clean between the petals and make small ruffles.

16

Fit the center section into the sanded middle section. If the two sections do not fit together snugly, keep working on the fit before proceeding to the next step. Look for thin areas by holding the middle section up to the light. Light will shine through the thinner areas.

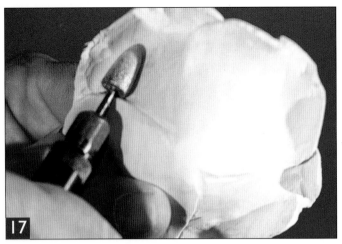

17

With a ruby taper, clean up underneath the petals and remove more of the waste wood.

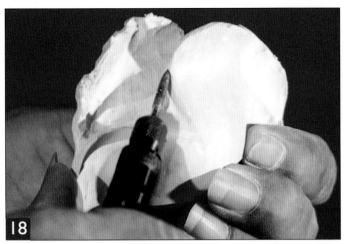

18

Use a diamond point to cut and clean the lines between the petals.

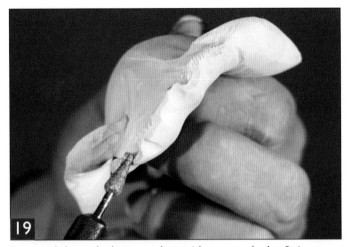

19

Form and shape the bottom edges with a tapered ruby. Strive to match the ruffles on the top edges of the petals.

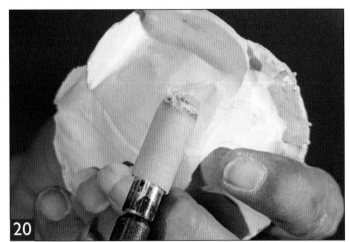

20

Use 220-grit sandpaper to clean and smooth the undersides of the petals.

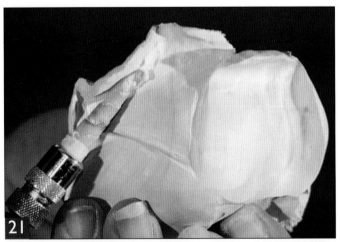

21

Use a tapered sander with 220-grit sandpaper to clean the areas you can't reach with the drum sander. Remember to hold the wood up to a strong light frequently to avoid sanding through thin areas.

Carving the Outer Section

This section will form the outer section of the rose. The middle and center sections will fit snugly into this last section. Again, patience in fitting the middle section into this outer section will reward you with a natural, pleasingly shaped flower. Frequent fittings and adjustments are necessary.

Be sure to vary the shapes of the petals as they are seen in nature.

Begin thinking now, how you want the sections you have just finished to fit into this last, outer section.

Study this photograph of the block and the carved middle section. It is important to understand the shape you are trying to achieve before you begin cutting.

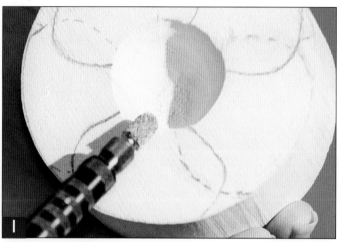

This section will have five petals. Number the petals and begin rounding out the center with the ball-nose Kutzall. You will be fitting the middle section here.

Before cutting any farther, plan how you want the middle section to fit into the outer section. Try to overlap the petals of the middle section over the outer section petals as much as possible.

When you have the sections positioned as you want them, make reference marks on both pieces.

Look at the block closely and decide how and where you need to remove wood to make the two sections fit.

5 Decide where the petals overlap and remove wood to separate the petals.

6 Form and shape each petal to fit the petal section above.

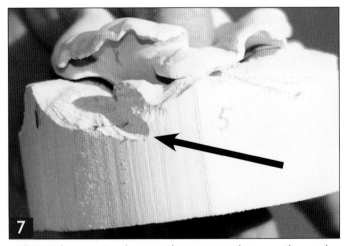

7 Make petal separation deeper to leave a space between the petals.

8 This photo shows five overlapping petals. Your piece should look like this before you proceed to the next step.

9 Using a drum sander with 220-grit sandpapeer, remove all of the Kutzall marks on the top of this section.

10 Fit the three pieces together to see if the sections are sitting low enough. From this angle, they look pretty good.

11 A side view shows that the sections are unfortunately not sitting low enough. Make the center hole deeper and lower the petals to create a better fit.

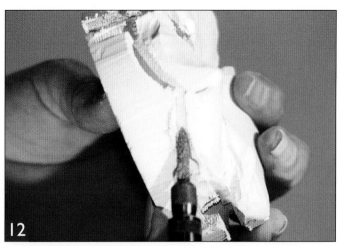

12 Cut a groove ¼ inch down from the top edges of the petals. Remove the wood on the sides of the petals with a tapered Kutzall. See Steps 5 to 8 of cutting the center section for tips on accomplishing this step.

13 Remember to allow for overlap when cutting away the wood on the side of each petal.

14 Cut away the excess waste wood. Taper down toward the center of the outer section.

15 With the Kutzall you can take off larger pieces of wood without the fear of breaking through the flower.

16 Check the bottom of your flower. The underside of the outer section should look like this before you continue to the next step.

17 Use a ball-nosed Kutzall to shape the underside of the petals and the center nub on the bottom.

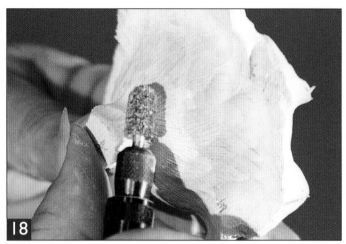

18 Continue to shape the underside of the petals with the ball-nosed Kutzall.

19 Strive to keep the gentle bowl shape on the underside of the petals. Add a contour roll to the petal edges.

20 Use a drum sander with 220-grit sandpaper to clean up the underside of the flower.

21 With a pointed tapered ruby, carefully clean up between the edges of the petals.

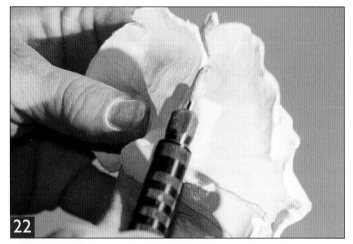

22 Take a pointed diamond and make the lines that form the individual petals on the bottom of the rose. Take these lines all the way down to the nub.

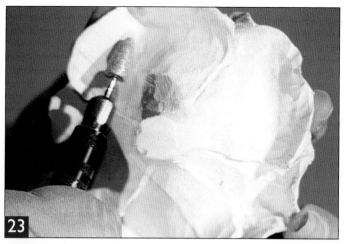

Change to the tapered ruby and clean up the underside of the flower.

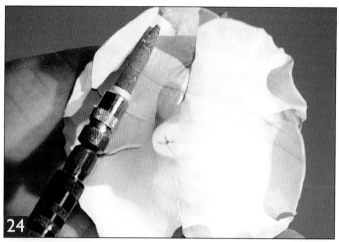

Continue cleaning up and finalizing the shape under the petals with a tapered sander using 400-grit sandpaper.

Do a final clean up on the rose with 400-grit sandpaper. Note how the three pieces fit together quite naturally.

A three-quarter view of the finish-carved rose shows how the three pieces fit nicely together.

Carving the Leaves

27

Use real leaves or the patterns on page 39. Trace the leaves onto ½-inch-thick tupelo wood. Cut the shapes out on a band saw or a scroll saw.

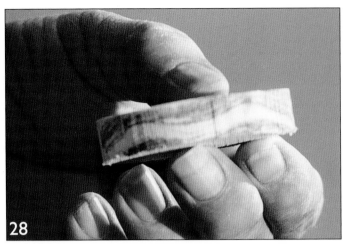

28

The sides of the leaf should not be flat. Sketch in a gentle movement to each leaf.

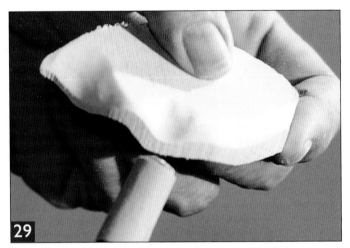

29

Use a drum sander with 220-grit sandpaper to add rolls to the leaves.

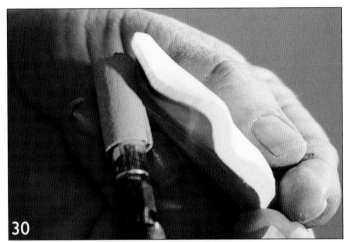

30

Repeat the rolling shapes on the bottom of the leaf. Try to match the shapes on the bottom as closely as possible to the shapes on the top.

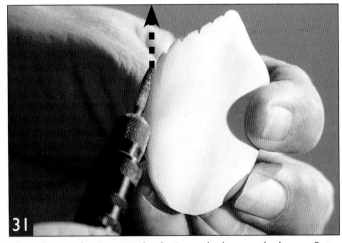

31

Use a diamond point to make the jagged edges on the leaves. Put the point of the bur in and pull up to make the edge.

32

Make the veins in the leaves by laying the diamond point on its side and pulling in a steady outward motion. Do not try to "write" the lines with the tip of the bit.

33 Repeat the previous step on the underside of the leaf.

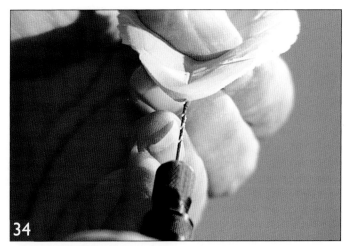

34 Drill a ³⁄₆₄-inch bit hole in the connecting edge of the leaf.

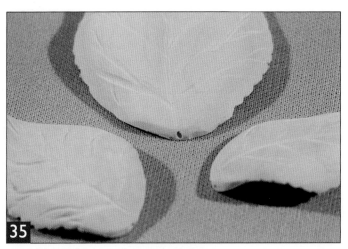

35 This photo shows three leaves in progress.

36 Insert a ³⁄₆₄-inch brass rod into each leaf. Do not glue the leaves until they have been painted.

37 Plan your display. I like to mount my roses on drift wood. You might like to try placing your rose in a vase or grouping several roses.

Painting the Flower

Roses come in a myriad of colors: reds, whites, yellows, even lavendars. You can paint your rose any color you want as long as you have three basic tones. Each rose must have a medium tone, a shadow and a highlight.

Paint three base coats and allow each coat to dry before painting the next coat. Throughout the process of painting, shading and highlighting the rose, your brush strokes should move from the center toward the edges of the petals and from the edges of the petals toward the center. Do not make any cross-over strokes. Assemble the following materials and paints before you begin:

- narrow flat brush
- wide flat brush
- #0/#10 liner brush
- super glue
- Krylon matte spray
- Jo Sonja acrylic paints (listed at right)

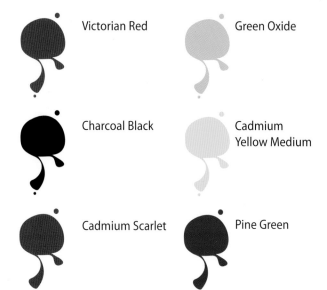

Victorian Red   Green Oxide

Charcoal Black   Cadmium Yellow Medium

Cadmium Scarlet   Pine Green

1 Paint three base coat washes of victorian red over the entire flower.

2 Add enough charcoal to the Victorian red to make a shadow wash. Paint the recessed areas of the center section and any edges where the petals fold. Blend while the last base coat is wet. If your paint dries out, wet it again for the best success.

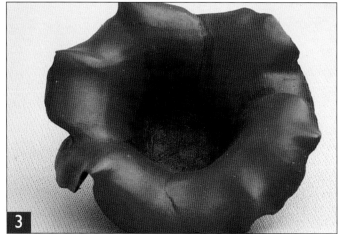

3 Repeat Step 2 on the middle section. Add a hint of cadmium yellow, straight from the tube, to a cadmium scarlet wash to make a highlight color. Remember to blend while the paint is still wet.

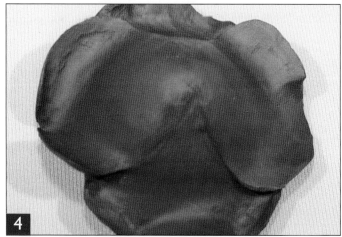

4 Darken the outer section with the wash of Victorian red and charcoal that you made in Step 2. The bowl shape and petal edges should be darkened as shown.

5 Highlight all three sections by drybrushing a mixture of cadmium scarlet and a hint of cadmium yellow medium.

6 Allow the paint to dry completely and assemble the flower. Use five-minute epoxy for assembly. This seems to hold better than super glue. Put a small amount of the epoxy in the bottom of the two outer sections and assemble. Be sure to take time to line up the flower sections so they fit as you carved them to fit.

7 Base coat all of the leaves with pine green. Highlight the leaves with cadmium yellow medium. Do a light wash of oxide green on the bottom of each leaf.

8 Using green oxide, trace the veins with a liner brush. Base coat the wires with all-purpose sealer and paint them pine green. Attach the leaves with super glue.

9 The painted, assembled flower.

10 Spray the finished flower and leaves with Krylon matte finish. (See more photos of the finished rose on page 3.)

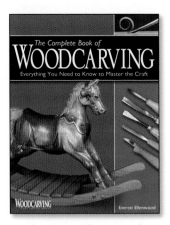

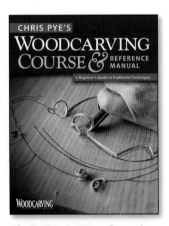

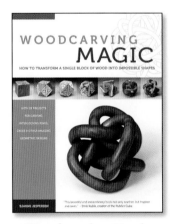
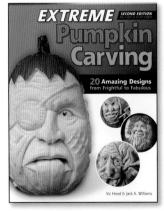
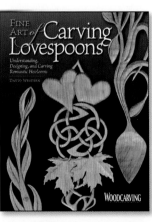
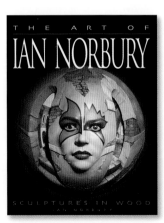

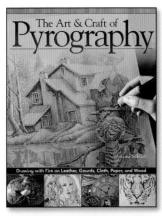

The Art & Craft of Pyrography
ISBN 978-1-56523-478-9 **$19.95**

Learn to Burn
ISBN 978-1-56523-728-5 **$16.99**

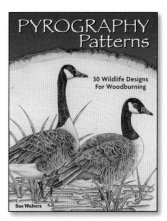

Pyrography Patterns
ISBN 978-1-56523-819-0 **$14.99**

**Woodburning Project
& Pattern Treasury**
ISBN 978-1-56523-482-6 **$24.95**

Pyrography Basics
ISBN 978-1-57421-505-2 **$9.99**

Woodburning with Style
ISBN 978-1-56523-443-7 **$24.95**

Great Book of Woodburning
ISBN 978-1-56523-287-7 **$22.95**

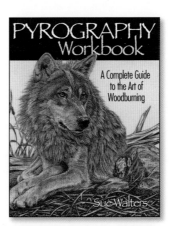

Pyrography Workbook
ISBN 978-1-56523-258-7 **$19.95**

**Great Book of Floral
Patterns, Second Edition**
ISBN 978-1-56523-447-5 **$24.95**

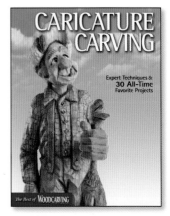
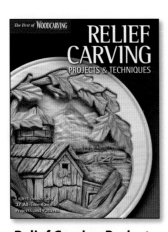